Yellow Everywhere

Kristin Sterling

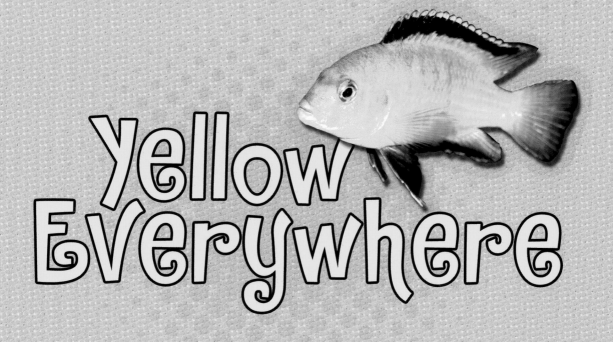

Lerner Publications Company
Minneapolis

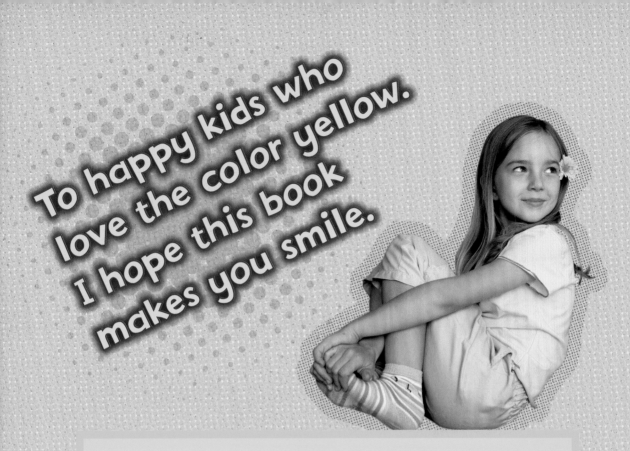

To happy kids who
love the color yellow.
I hope this book
makes you smile.

Lerner Publications Company
A division of Lerner Publishing Group, Inc.
241 First Avenue North
Minneapolis, MN 55401 U.S.A.

Website address: www.lernerbooks.com

Library of Congress Cataloging-in-Publication Data

    Yellow everywhere / by Kristin Sterling.
      p.   cm. — (Lightning bolt books™—Colors everywhere)
    Includes index.
    ISBN 978-0-7613-4589-3 (lib. bdg. : alk. paper)
    1. Yellow—Juvenile literature. 2. Colors—Juvenile literature. I. Title.
QC495.5.S7495 2010
535.6—dc22   2009017951

Manufactured in the United States of America
1 — BP — 12/15/09

Contents

A Cheerful World

Do you like bright, sunny colors? Many people love the color yellow.

The world around
you is full of
yellow things.

The sun is yellow as it sets in the sky. It gives the world light and heat.

This father and son fly a kite on the beach as the sun goes down.

Bananas turn yellow as they ripen. You know a banana is ready to be eaten when it is yellow.

Sunflowers have yellow petals. The buds of these flowers face east in the morning and west in the evening.

Chicks are tiny yellow balls of fluff soon after they hatch from eggs. They change color as they grow.

This baby chick is wet because it just hatched. It will dry and become fluffy like the others.

Bumblebees are black and yellow. They fly around collecting nectar in gardens.

Mustard is a dark yellow seed.

It is made into a topping for hot dogs and hamburgers.

Do you like to eat hot dogs with mustard?

People also make things that are yellow.

Some cars are a sunny yellow color.

Have you ever ridden in a yellow car?

This traffic light is about to turn red.

Yellow lights tell people to slow down.

Shades of Yellow

Many shades of yellow can be found in the world. They range from light yellow to dark yellow.

Canary yellow is a bright shade of yellow.

Canaries are birds. Some people keep this kind of bird as a pet.

These kitchen walls are butter yellow. This color is soft and calm.

The living room is golden yellow. This color is warm and dark.

This grandmother and granddaughter enjoy reading in their living room.

Chartreuse is a yellow green shade. This pear is chartreuse.

Is yellow Mellow?

How does the color yellow make you feel? Some people think it is a mellow and relaxing color.

Others feel it is happy and energizing. They feel cheerful when they see it.

Yellow ribbons are a sign of hope during a war.

People wear yellow ribbons to show support for soldiers who are far away.

Yestera Loves Yellow

Yestera loves the color yellow.
It makes her feel happy.

She likes to paint with primary colors. She mixes yellow, red, and blue to create other colors.

She mixes yellow with blue to make green. Yellow and red make orange.

If you add white to yellow and red, you'll get a light shade of orange.

25

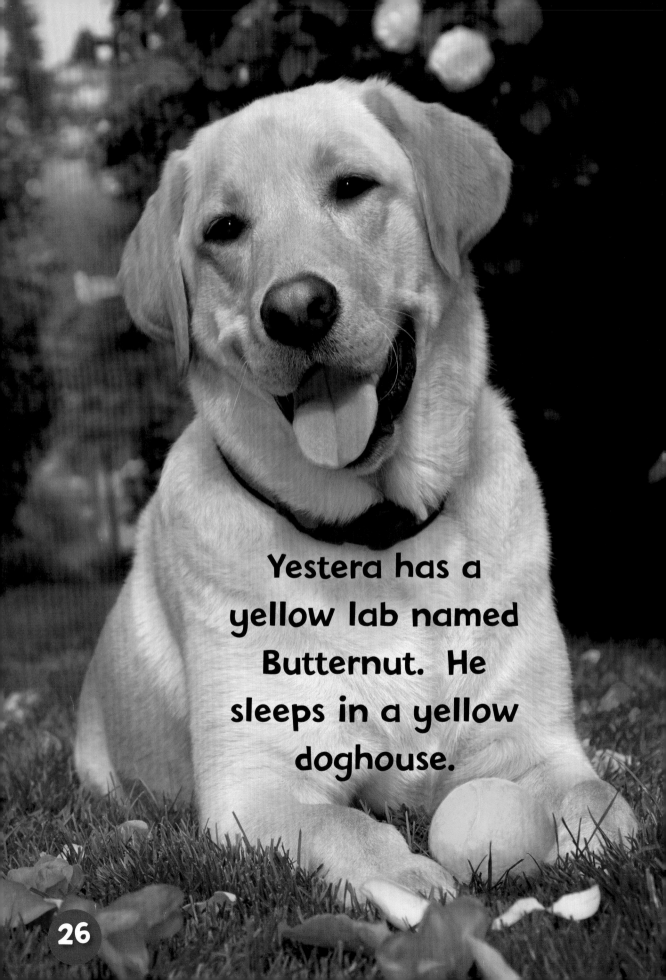

Yestera has a yellow lab named Butternut. He sleeps in a yellow doghouse.

What is your favorite color?

27

Activity
You Can Make a Rainbow

Do you like rainbows? They are created when light hits small raindrops in the air. You can make your own rainbow with a few supplies.

What you need:
water
a clear drinking glass
masking tape
a flashlight
a sheet of white paper
a notebook
a pencil

What you do:

1. Pour water almost to the top of the drinking glass.

2. Place two pieces of masking tape on the flashlight so the light shines through a narrow slit.

3. Place the glass near the edge of a counter or table. Put the sheet of white paper on the floor near the counter.

4. Turn off the lights to make the room darker.

5. Shine the flashlight through the glass and down toward the paper. You will see a rainbow appear on the paper.

6. Move the flashlight up and down and side to side. Does the rainbow move on the paper? Try moving the flashlight closer to the glass and then farther away. Does the size of the rainbow change? Write down what you notice in the notebook.

Glossary

hatch: to come out of an egg

mellow: laid back

nectar: a sweet liquid produced by flowers

primary color: a color that cannot be made by mixing other colors

ripen: to grow and become ready to be eaten

Further Reading

Color Mixing
http://www.enchantedlearning.com/crafts/
Colormixing.shtml

Light and Color
http://scifiles.larc.nasa.gov/kids/Problem_Board/
problems/light/sim1.html

Ross, Kathy. *Kathy Ross Crafts Colors.*
Minneapolis: Millbrook Press, 2003.

Van Gogh, Vincent. *Vincent's Colors.* San
Francisco: Chronicle Books, 2005.

Weather Wiz Kids
http://www.weatherwizkids.com/weather-optical-
illusions.htm

Yolen, Jane. *Color Me a Rhyme.* Honesdale, PA:
Boyds Mills Press, 2000.

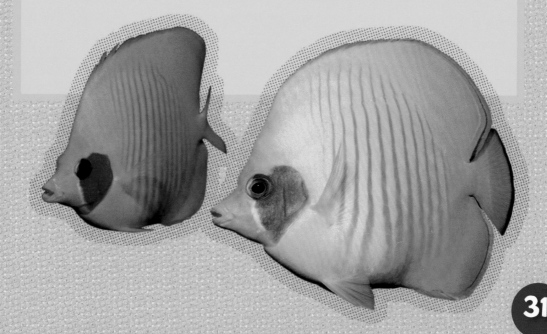

Index

Photo Acknowledgments

The images in this book are used with the permission of: © Vladimir Sakharov/
Dreamstime.com, p. 1; © Paul Vozdic/Iconica/Getty Images, p. 2; © Mauritius/
Photolibrary, p. 4; © Debra Boast/Dreamstime.com, p. 5; © Chuck Fishman/The Image
Bank/Getty Images, p. 6; © Photononstop/SuperStock, p. 7; © Royalty-Free/CORBIS,
p. 8; © age fotostock/SuperStock, p. 9; © Rosemary Calvert/SuperStock, p. 10; © Jose
Luiz Pelaez/Iconica/Getty Images, p. 11; © Drive Images/Alamy, p. 12; © Altrendo
Images/Getty Images, p. 13; © David Cobb/Alamy, p. 14; © Icholakov/Dreamstime.com,
p. 15; © Starletdarlene/Dreamstime.com, p. 16; © Rob Melnychuk/Photodisc/Getty
Images, p. 17; © Flavia Raddavero/Dreamstime.com, p. 18; © Flying Colours Ltd/Digital
Vision/Getty Images, p. 19; © Frazer Cunningham/Iconica/Getty Images, p. 20;
© iStockphoto.com/Gary Woodard, p. 21; © Kablonk!/Photolibrary, p. 22; © Jim
Corwin/Photographer's Choice/Getty Images, p. 23; © Jeff Smith/Photographer's
Choice/Getty Images, p. 24; © Ableimages/Riser/Getty Images, p. 25; © Troy Klebey/
Photographer's Choice/Getty Images, p. 26; © Kate Connell/Photonica/Getty Images,
p. 27; © Todd Strand/Independent Picture Service, p. 28; © Karl Weatherly/Photodisc/
Getty Images, p. 30; © Reinhard Dishcherl/SuperStock, p. 31.
Cover: © Rozaliya/Dreamstime.com (sunflower); © Py2000/Dreamstime.com (school
bus); © Ene/Dreamstime.com (canary); © Leonid Konnov/Dreamstime.com (corn);
© Lgrig/Dreamstime.com (banana); © Todd Strand/Independent Picture Service
(paint strips).